Church Security 1.0

MW00914804

Preface: In 2005 four of us, realizing the need for an Emergency Response Team, joined together on our quest. Blind as bats but having a modicum of individual experience, we launched. The four of us, a former FBI Intelligence analyst, a U.S. Navy Submarine Officer, a former Deputy Sheriff and a carpenter set about to safeguard a "Mega" church that sees over 500,000 people a year, through various services and community outreach. *What were we thinking?*

In time we were joined by a variety of members with as many backgrounds. At the time of this writing (2018) there are over 85 dedicated men and women with the "spirit of Nehemiah and the soul of a Sheepdog" on our Team. Being a "Mega" church has its challenges. Size is one, certainly, but we have found through sharing our experience that size really doesn't matter. The Christian Church is under attack. Large or small we all have the same issues, thus this booklet.

My prayer is that the information contained in this brief publication will help and inspire you to build a church emergency response team based on the experience of those who have gone before you.

History: Since 1999 through 2017 over 1,700 deadly force attacks have been launched against churches and synagogues in the United States. These attacks have resulted in 617 deaths with innumerable serious injuries. It is estimated also that there have been eight times as many sexual assaults on church property in that same period of time.[1] (over 13,000). This information is, sadly, updated weekly at www.carlchinn.com.

Whether your church is a "mega" church or a home church or somewhere in between, this e-book is written to give you some ideas on how to protect the "flock" for we are Sheepdogs and that is our mission.

---

[1] www.carlchinn.com

Biblical references: Are found throughout the Bible but my "go to" is Nehemiah 4:9 *"We prayed to our God and posted a guard…"* He does not want us to be undefended. He wants His people to worship in safety and in peace, so in Luke 22:36, He encourages us to *"sell your cloak, and purchase a sword (read weapon)."*

The Emergency Response Team (ERT) is the modern equivalent of the Praetorian Guard of ancient Rome or Temple Guards of ancient Jerusalem. The team member attempts to anticipate threats to the pastor or congregants and to avoid them, but if the threat cannot be avoided and turns up with a weapon in its hand a few feet away, the security person's reflexes, skills, actions, training and equipment may dictate the need to engage and neutralize the threat. That takes training, training and more training.

LTC David Grossman, USA, Ret., writes in his paper, ***"On Sheep, Wolves and Sheepdogs,"*** that there are three kinds of people. In this writing he points out that "Most of the people in our society are sheep. They are kind, gentle, productive creatures who can only hurt one another by accident. Wolves, on the other hand, feed on the sheep without mercy. Do you believe there are wolves out there who will feed on the flock without mercy? You better believe it. There are evil people in this world and they are capable of evil deeds. The moment you forget that or pretend it is not so, you become a sheep. There is no safety in denial."[2]

According to the FBI, the murder rate currently in the U.S. is six per 100,000 per year, and the aggravated assault rate is four per 1,000 per year. What this means is that the vast majority of Americans are not inclined to hurt one another. Some estimates say that two million Americans are victims of violent crimes every year, a tragic, staggering number, perhaps an all-time record rate of violent crime.[3] But there are over 300 million Americans, which means that the odds of being a victim of violent crime is considerably less than one in a hundred in any given year. Furthermore, since many violent crimes are

---

[2] Sheep, Wolves and Sheepdogs by LTC David Grossman, USA Ret
[3] Crime Statistics, FBI

committed by repeat offenders, the actual number of violent citizens is considerably less than two million.[4]

"Then there are sheepdogs," he went on, "and I'm a sheepdog. I live to protect the flock and confront the wolf."

As noted above, deadly force incidents in churches, though a lesser number, is still well above what we should expect in a place where we would and should expect peace.

What can you do? My prayer is that the following will help to guide you.

Rule number 1: Start with what you have.

Rule number 2: Don't hang so much on the boat that it sinks.

Rule Number 3: This is a Ministry, not a police department.

In the Beginning

Sheepdogs: How do you build a Team? It's an anointing. We are called to protect the flock and confront the wolf. Look for volunteers with backgrounds in first response (Police, Fire, EMS), military, nursing or folks with that First Responder down deep inside just itching to come out, and then help them. And, they need to be prayer warriors.

Ask Questions

1. Why does the person want to be on the Emergency Response Team?
2. Is the person faithful to the Church and to his/her family?
3. Does the person get along well with others?
4. Is the person conscientious
5. Can the person be discrete?
6. Us the person physically fit?

---

[4] "On Killing" by LTC David Grossman

7. Can the person pass a criminal background check? (I am always amazed at the number of folks who never get back to me with the form. It's almost like asking for a candidate for a urine analysis.)

Beware of those who have a CWP (Concealed Weapons Permit) as their only background and are more than anxious to carry their gun in church. This is a red flag. We have met folks like that. In our state (SC), a CWP only means that there was no open warrant on the day that he/she applied. My guess is that it is the same where you are. The training is minimum and authority to act beyond self-protection (or that of others) doesn't exist, nor does follow up training. You must expand this training. Express pastoral or executive level permission must also be granted to anyone who carries on church property in SC. (If this is you, make sure that you have that permission **in writing**. Words are cheap and a court won't acknowledge just words.)

A proper mindset for the protection of others is the base upon which you build a team of "sheepdogs." Mindset accounts for 80% of your priority in any high-risk endeavor. Then you add basic skills, tactics and equipment. "The proper protection of your church leadership and of the congregation requires a specific set of skills, principal among which is mindset. We start with the premise that if we have a dedicated person on the Team, then all of the rest of the skills, tactics, etc., become a lot easier to deal with. If a person doesn't have the mindset, he/she may not be in the right ministry."[5]

Patrick Lencioni's book *"The Ideal Team Player"* encourages us to look for people with the heart of a servant, one who is "humble, hungry and smart." "Humble is pretty obvious, we can't abide big egos. Hungry is all about working hard, being passionate about the work (and looking for ways to serve). Smart has to do with being aware of the people around you and dealing with them in a positive, (and appropriate) functional way." [6]They must have a cool head in an emergency, or when faced with imminent danger, slow to anger and

---

[5] "Defending the Flock" by Kris Maloney
[6] "The Ideal Team Player" by Patrick Lencioni

well prepared.

Training roles and responsibilities

We train our team members to look for people in the crowd who are roaming and canvassing rather than lingering and interacting. We call it DLR (Don't Look Right). Offer assistance and watch for the reaction. Make notes. (If you have concerns, note the physical description of the person in question, the license number and vehicle description. Use your cell phone camera option.) Look for <u>unfamiliar behaviors</u> in those people you both know and don't know. Stay alert and aware, but friendly. Remember this is <u>not</u> a police department, it is a <u>ministry</u> of your church. Engage people in conversation, especially if you have not seen them before. You may find it is simply a person who is in need of individual prayer or having an unusually difficult week; we all have them. Make a note, and always smile…but maintain a safe distance and <u>watch their hands</u>.

Learn the difference between a need to call for the care ministry and to call the police. This isn't always a simple decision. Most are aware of the obvious calls; theft, assault, threats to others and to self. Actions, which break the law, require intervention by the police. On the other hand, people are fragile and their emotions can be unpredictable. Crisis situations do occur, especially within a religious body. Know what to look for. Irrational thinking, extreme behaviors, casual or subtle threats against themselves or others…all can indicate potential security threats. Drugs, alcohol and stress can trigger behaviors which are potentially harmful. The book, ***"Left of Bang,"*** is very helpful. Written by two former USMC Officers, it is a primer on combat profiling but works in all scenarios to help you to recognize potential problems. (If 12:00 is the problem (Bang) then 1:00, 2:00 and 3:00 is when help arrives. We want to live <u>left</u> of Bang, at 10:00 or 11:00; <u>before</u> it happens.)

Have frequent training meetings and opportunities, monthly at a minimum, to bring in new members and to review the issues at your church and others with whom you have relationships. If appropriate, start meeting with other church teams, at least their leadership, to share ideas possible threats and training. Consider adding the local school security people to this group. We are all dealing with the same community issues.

Structure: Depending on the size of your team, train up leaders so that you have depth for the future. In a "mega" church where there may be several dozen ERT Members, there should be a Team Leader for every ten Members so that leadership isn't trying to communicate to too many people. The days of multi-site are upon us and teams are being established in the outlying campuses. They will all need leaders and uniformity in training. ***"The Ideal Team Player"*** is a great guide for member and leader selection.

Risk Assessment: Risk can be divided into categories; internal/external and intangible. Internal risks are threats inside of the facility. For example, marriage counseling can degrade into domestic violence. Situational awareness dictates that parking lot escorts may be required. Locked doors, adequate lighting, and cameras are all necessary ways to reduce risk. This may help: Short_Security_Assessment_v2.pdf

Adequate lighting, both inside and outside will provide the number one deterrent to criminal activity. Access control to all areas of the facility and the ability to lock down areas where children are located (in case of an active shooter, for example) should be mandatory.

Cameras: Cameras are a great, and necessary, accessory to your Security System. They are somewhat of a deterrent but more importantly they can document an incident if something happens, and act as a warning to those bent on wrongdoing. Make certain that you purchase HD cameras, movement activated with at least two weeks of memory. If possible, and this is the best scenario, have someone monitor the cameras during services. The placement of these cameras is very important. The obvious places are doorways, hallways, (outside of lavatories is prime because of sexual attacks) tithe deposit locations, worship center and don't forget the classrooms and the parking lot.

The estimate from Carl Chinn is that 75% of the attacks on churches initiate on the parking lot and 60% happen when there are no services going on. Make certain that you have protection on these fronts and that your church offices are protected.[7]

Carl's book, ***"Evil Invades the Sanctuary"*** is what we use as an introduction to church security. Carl was the security member on duty when Focus on the Family was attacked and again when New Life Church in Colorado Springs was attacked. (The bullet hole is still visible in the wall at the main building of Focus on the Family!) His experience is priceless for all of us who are called to this ministry. His book will give you a picture of what happened before, during and after.

We also encourage the reading of a variety of books listed later, but ***"Defending the Flock"*** by Kris Maloney is certainly a good basic text to help you start a program or refine what you have.

Member Identification: Each Member of the Emergency Response Team should be marked so that in an emergency the staff can locate them. Our church uses red lanyards with cards that read "Emergency" on them. For Member safety, these lanyards have a release mechanism in the back so that the lanyard cannot be used to choke out the wearer. "Security" banners from DSM Safety Banners are worn in belt holsters or pocket cases in case of extreme emergency. These banners have been proven by the FBI to be the safest thing to wear during an Active Shooter incident to prevent "friendly" fire accidents. They are only deployed in emergencies.

Equipment: Each Member should carry, at a minimum, a note pad, pen, small flashlight and pocketknife. If armed, his/her weapon in a sturdy level two holster, two additional magazines of ammunition, examination gloves and a tourniquet. We do not allow shoulder holsters or SOB (Small of the Back) holsters or the SERPA with a trigger retention release. There is too much "sweep" when the weapon is drawn from the shoulder holster or the small of the

---

[7] www.carlchinn.com

back and the trigger release types present accidental discharge possibilities, nay, probabilities.

Medical: Enlist any medical professionals within your congregation with the heart for emergency service. Have adequate emergency medical supplies on hand to care for multiple trauma injuries. "Israeli" compression bandages are quite good, as well as chest seals and have lots of tourniquets. A small first aid kit for minor injuries is also suggested as a separate item. Plan for the worst, hope for the best.

Depending on the size of your church you should consider placing trauma kits in various locations around the building. A "stop the bleed" training program should be part of your ongoing training. Regardless of the form of attack or the simple incident, if blood is flowing it must be stopped. An arterial bleed will last about 20 seconds before it is too late. Your local EMS is a good place to start for training and FEMA also offers a course through the Department of Homeland Security. (stopthebleed@hq.dhs.gov).

Recognizing the Threat

DLR (Don't Look Right)

Again, (it's worth a repeat) look for unfamiliar people who are roaming and canvassing, rather than parking and interacting. Offer assistance and notice their reactions. Make notes. Look for unfamiliar behaviors in those people you both know and don't know. Stay alert and always aware of your surroundings. Engage the person if possible in conversation. You may find that it is simply a person who is in need of individual prayer or having a difficult time. Make notes.

Learn the difference between the need to call for ministry and the need to call for the police. This is not always a simple decision. The obvious calls— theft, assault, threats to self or others—require intervention by police. On the other side, people are fragile, and their emotions can be unpredictable. Crisis situations do occur, especially within the church body. Know what to look/listen for: irrational thinking, extreme behaviors, casual or subtle threats against themselves or others, all can indicate potential threats. Drugs, alcohol and stress can also trigger behaviors that are potentially harmful.

Your work will be easier if you form a good working relationship with your local police and EMS personnel. When in doubt, call the professionals. Make sure that your cell phone has their numbers programmed. Offer your building for training.

- Know your legal responsibilities and liabilities.

- Know how to write a report based on your observations.

- Know the church Emergency Plan.

Generally, attacks are prefaced by signals of aggression and ritualized combat. Some early behavior warning signals and pre-attack clues which may indicate that an attack is imminent would include:

- Face turns red on fair-skinned people

- Head, shoulders and strong side drop back

- Subject uses a target glance at the person

- Subject uses a directional look

- Excessive salivation such as spitting

- Breathing quicker and deeper

- Sweating; looks through you (1,000 yard stare)

- Subject gets belligerent, challenging, yelling, cursing, etc.

- Exaggerated movements (pacing, finger pointing, hands on hips, balled fists.)

- Stands as tall as possible

- Redirects aggression on an inanimate object

- Lips tighten over the teeth

- Verbalization stops, hands set, head and shoulders drop down.

Types of Threats:

- Verbal assaults

- Thrown objects

- Physical attacks

- Concealed weapons

How they come:

- Deranged, Suicidal, Physically Abused

- Disgruntled, Emotional, Psychological Issues

- Criminals

- Handicapped, Mentally Challenged

- Homeless

Law Enforcement: (LEO) Having a good relationship with the local police is very important. Your work will be made easier that way. Many churches hire off-duty officers for traffic control and some have them in plain clothes inside the building. Learn their local number and program it into your cell phone. Many of the 911 systems are regional and it may take longer for the dispatch to make good things happen. Land lines are faster because the location of the incoming call is identified to the dispatcher. Cell phones do not do this. Remember, when trouble is seconds away, the police are minutes away.

If you do contract with them they should:

- Maintain professional demeanor, stay alert and off of their cell phones.

- Remain at assigned posts prior to, during, and after services.

- Observe for hazardous events and dangerous or suspicious individuals

- Provide assistance to Church staff in dealing with incidents or individuals who are disruptive to the service or cause a safety concern for members and visitors.

- All officers are to respond to events and occurrences with the level of force consistent with the policies of the police department they are employed by.

The volunteer members are there to assist the active police officers and not to take a primary role, unless forced into that position. Have a plan. The ERT shall act as force multipliers, as needed, in any incident. (If an ambulance is needed, the police can get one faster through 911 than a civilian can, so have them do it if they are available.)

More on Training

Active Shooter: The last time a child perished in a school fire was in December of 1958, at Our Lady of The Angels in Chicago, IL. And yet schools conduct fire drills monthly in government mandated fire retardant buildings. Are they necessary? Yes, but they certainly need modification to today's threats.

At this writing (9/10/2018), the most recent child that died as a result of a school shooting was on 14 February 2018 in Florida where 17 perished. Of all of the 160 Active Shooter incidents recorded between 2000 and 2013, only 68 involved churches. This does not lessen the need for training on how to react.

"When the moment of truth arrives, the time for preparation has passed."
CDR Mike Mercer, USN (Ret)

ALICE offers some excellent on-line training if there isn't any alternative in your area. Contact www.alicetraining.com for information.

Active Shooter drills should be done if possible, especially with your staff. Learning how to Run, Hide or Fight takes thought and practice. Monthly training is encouraged. Use the time to walk through the various rooms and places on your property that could be susceptible to attack and begin to formulate your response. Do not assume that every member of your team is on the same page when it comes to deadly response. Drills will begin to cause the "cream" to rise to the top. Grossman's book "On Killing" is an excellent reference. An interactive drill will help with a "gut check."

Check YouTube for videos produced by several agencies on how to handle an Active Shooter incident. Understand that if it occurs, people die every three seconds and the incident is usually over in five minutes. How long will it take for your police to respond? Are you prepared to engage? Do you know how? Do you understand the risks involved. Is it time for a gut check? In the June, 2018, attack in Annapolis, MD, the police arrived within one minute of the alarm and the shooter was still able to kill six and wound almost a dozen! There were over 170 people in that building. How many were saved by the rapid (and very unusual) response of law enforcement?

Defensive tactics: "To win without fighting is best."[8]   But if you have a martial art practitioner available, employ him/her to teach your team some simple defensive moves; it could save lives and a lot of trouble. Practice these tactics quarterly at a minimum. No Karate chops, no rolling around on the floor, work on deflection and compliance holds.

There is a right way and a wrong way to restrain a person. The correct way minimizes injury to both you and the person being restrained. Although few and far between, occasionally the need for restraint does arise. And most

---

[8] "The Art of War" by Sun Tzu

commonly this occurs when one person is attempting to harm another person. Don't stand in the middle! This will not secure the threat. It will only make you the target and once you are down the threat continues. Most fights last less than three minutes, so if there is one, protect the perimeters and be patient. If needed, get trained in the use of handcuffs or "Flex-cuffs" by your local police. Training and the documentation of the training is vital to support your actions if the need for justification should ever arise.

Do not use any equipment (handcuffs, pepper spray, baton, firearm) that you have not been certified to use. You will only get into trouble.

Firearms: If concealed firearms are authorized, frequent practice must be required. Your State law will dictate rules on concealed weapons in churches. Monthly practice, logged into a book to maintain discipline should be mandated. You will need to document your training should an incident occur. I strongly encourage you to use the either the FBI firearms qualification as your base or your state's law enforcement qualifications. Either one should require 50 rounds in a B-1 target at varying ranges from 3 to 25 yards. Certainly go beyond the minimum if possible. Weapons proficiency is a diminishing skill. Practice, practice, practice and document it. We also require each carrying Member to have membership in USCCA for their personal protection. Regardless of the justification of your actions, there will be a civil suit. Can you or your team members afford the costs? Get the insurance. Check and see if an IDPA match is held in your area. The move and shoot training within these matches is priceless.

Communication: Select radios which will work in your facility. Be aware that construction materials and distance can have a deleterious effect on transmissions and receptions. Depending on the size of your facility a repeater may be required. We currently have over 250,000 square feet under the roof on 44 acres. We have two repeaters and a digital system. You may be able to do quite well with a set of "family" radios but make sure they come with ear pieces for a less conspicuous look. Most importantly, make sure that they work on your property.

Mental Health: There isn't much help for those suffering from mental disorders from the government. Consult with your local health department for suggestions and/or direction. In some states, disrupting a church service is a misdemeanor regardless of mental condition. Law Enforcement should deal with these issues. In most cases, unless your church is willing and able to take on the heavy ministry required, a Trespass notice should be issued and the courts decide what to do with the individual. Protection of the Flock is paramount in all cases. Share the information carefully with other church security leaders in your area. These folks tend to migrate to other Houses of Worship when they are banned from one.

Domestic Issues: Divorce cases and child custody issues can cause problems in several areas. Attacks on pastoral staff due to counseling are a leading cause of these attacks. A disagreeable spouse, assuming that the church has taken the side of opposing spouse, can erupt into violence (remember, 60% of attacks happen during non-church services). [9] These usually happen during the week but we have had unhappy spouses show up during services demanding access to their children. You need to be ready for that and have a plan.

Children's Ministry: Divorce cases can manifest all sorts of bad actions on the part of very peaceful people. A thoughtful system of check-in and check-out must be established to assure that the child is under the supervision of the proper parent.

Despite whimsical names like the Butterfly Room or the Puppy Room, officials take the safety of children seriously. Reporting mandates have recently changed. Check your state regulations and do not ignore them. Extensive background checks on teachers will also help parents to feel more comfortable (only 10% of child abusers are ever actually caught).[10] Dropping their children off when they know that a check-in and check-out system is in place and that cameras are in place to make parents feel secure. We use a three tag system; one on the child, one on the parent and one in a book, all issued when the child checks in. To pick the child up three tags must match in the book.

---

[9] www.carlchinn.com
[10] www.ministrysafe.com

The ERT officer assigned to the Children's area should focus on the safety of the children and staff in the Kids areas. The ERT officer must maintain a position near the check-in/check-out and monitor the crowd.

• No person is allowed into the children's ministry area without an appropriate Kids Ministry sticker.

• This assigned officer must remain at the post as long as there are children under the care of church staff or volunteers.

• This assigned officer's primary responsibility is the safety of the children, church members, visitors, and staff in the children's area.

• The staff will be the assigned officer's guide as to whether or not a child is allowed to leave the area with someone.

• If the staff advises the assigned officer that an individual does not meet the requirement to pick up a child, the officer will not allow the child to leave until the staff agrees to release the child.

• Any event or suspicious person the assigned officer notices that is outside the children's area should be reported to other officers so they can handle the matter, so that he/she can remain on post.

The exception to this is if the event or person is dangerous or life threatening and requires immediate action. The officer should advise other officers of the event and then respond to the event. We suggest the *"Ministry Safe"* (www.ministrysafe.com) group out of Ft Worth, TX. Their training is excellent. Also look at "Darkness to Light" at www.d2l.org.

Pastoral Protection: The most important member of your church is the Pastor. He/she is usually the biggest target as well. Each church building is different, so you will have to look at all of the angles of possible attack, perhaps role-play an attack by gun, by knife and by physical attack to see where the best points of protection might be.

When you set up a Pastoral Protection Detail (PPD), you will need the Pastor's participation. Learn to cover without smothering, watch everyone's hands, learn to look for concealed weapons, and establish a system of communication between the PPD member and the protectee in case of someone monopolizing the him/her time or a perceived threat. We use the "Carol Burnette" (tug on the earlobe). When this signal is employed we move in and inform the pastor of an "important phone call" and move him/her along to a safe place. Employ this system for guest speakers as well. Treat them like VIP's, you never know who or when an attack can come or who the target could be.

Worship Team: They too need covering. There are "groupies" and there are those who may disagree with the form of music that you offer. Also, the instruments are very valuable and subject to theft or damage. We assign one ERT officer to watch them before and after each service. We have had stalkers and even had someone follow a musician home…twice!

VIP Protection: Our church hosts a sitting U.S. Senator almost every week and not everyone agrees with his politics. Politics being what they are today, we protect this person as if he were also a pastor. No one wants another Tucson, AZ or Arlington, VA incident, so I encourage you to plan VIP movements, learn "diamond" and "box" formations and have an escape plan. Never place the principal in the same place week after week and do not have marked parking spots for anyone.

Intelligence: Several years ago a father and son team, the Twittys, traveled for 12 years throughout the Southeast preying on churches with the same sob story of a sick mother and no money. The plate was passed and they moved on. The problem? There was no sick mother. They were able to get away with this scam for 12 years before they were caught because none of the churches talked to the others.

You should begin to establish relationships with area church security teams to share intelligence about possible criminal activity or disturbed folks who may go from church to church. Groups like the *Dancing Californians* or the *Westboro Baptists* will invade a church and defy anyone to touch them so that they can file suit against the church for assault. If they are in your area, you need to know about them. An Intel relationship will go a long way towards helping with this issue. Also, the FBI has a non-profit called "InfraGard." (**www.infragard.org**) This is a partnership between the FBI and the private sector. It is an association of persons who represent businesses, academic institutions, state and local law enforcement agencies, and other participants dedicated to sharing information and intelligence to prevent hostile acts against the United States." Faith-based is one of the groups through the Commercial Buildings silo. As important is membership in the Faith Based Security Network, (www.fbsnamerica.com). Either start a chapter or join a chapter near you.

Additional Training:

"We don't rise to the level of our expectations, we rise to the level of our training."

Archilochus (680-645 BC)

"The Sheepdogs," Carl Chinn, Jimmy Meeks and LTC Dave Grossman, travel the Nation presenting the need for church security and promoting the concept of the Sheepdog. You can get their schedule at www.sheepdogtraining.com. I encourage you to seek this out and attend one as soon as they are close to you. The statistics will impress you to move forward sooner than later, and the information presented can help to justify the need for security to your leadership if needed. They tell you why, but they don't tell you how. Only you know the culture and the physical layout of your church.

Kris Mahoney of *Sheepdog Church Security,* has developed a training system that will take you from zero to operational in short order. Available online (for a fee) you can download his Power Point teaching tools and lesson plans which can be modified to your program.

Kris has developed an online "school" to help you and your Team learn from scores of others who have gone before us. Titled *"Church Safety and*

Security Volunteer Academy." (www.sheepdogsecurity.com)

Tim Miller, Security Director at Christ Fellowship in FL, has developed a training program that we use. Similar to Mahoney's, but more targeted. We have a training meeting every month and fold these topics into a 17-20 hour training block to compliment our base training from SCSLED (see below). It includes:

1. ***Church Security, 101*:** One hour introduction that covers the differences between Law Enforcement, Security and Church Security. (actually part of our basic SLED training.)

2. ***Preparing the Mind and Body for Crisis*:** A one hour training based on the latest human performance studies for how to train the mind and body in advance in order to significantly improve the performance during a crisis. ***"The Gift of Fear"*** by Gavin DeBecker is a great primer for this class. As his tome ***"Two Seconds."*** You will be amazed how many critical incidents go down in two seconds.

3. ***Stop the Bleed*:** A two hour Emergency Medical Course developed by the Department of Homeland Security (DHS) to prepare people to save lives immediately following a crisis. This is practical and interactive and teaches how to apply a pressure bandage and tourniquets. You can become an instructor at:

    http://www.Stopthebleed@hq.dhs.gov

4. ***Basic Sanctuary Training*:** A two hour training block for the Ushers, Greeters, Staff and Security Team that details the security plan for the sanctuary and then interactively trains the teams for a variety of different scenarios (Fire, Weather, Protestors, Mentally Ill, Hecklers, Combative people, etc. How to patrol church buildings and grounds, and implement "situational awareness" techniques.

5. ***Security Awareness Training for Ushers, Greeters and the Parking Lot Team, and Basic Radio Procedures*:** This is a two hour training class designed to instruct our "First Touch" teams about their security responsibilities and how they can make a difference in helping to protect the church. This training is very practical and provides interactive

instruction for what to do if they encounter certain situations. Also a crash course on professional methods for using radio systems correctly should be injected here.

6. ***Tactical Sanctuary Training:*** Create specific operational policies and procedures for your church and its safety team. This is a two hour block exclusively for the ERT to learn and practice exactly what will happen should an active violence event occur in the sanctuary. This training can employ "air-soft" guns and ensures that our teams understand what to do should a violent person(s) enter the sanctuary by interactively responding to an event.

7. ***Dealing with the Mentally Ill:*** This is a three hour class from the National Association of Mental Illness (NAMI) based designed to provide practical instruction about how to identify and deal effectively with the mentally ill. Here are several links that you may find helpful in developing a plan.

http://www.nami.org/Get-involved/NAMI-FaithNet/Tips-For-How-to-Help-a-Person-with-Mentalillness

http://www.asmfmh.org/resources/publications/tips-on-communicating-with-a-mentallyt-ill-person/

https://www.psychologytoday.com/us/blog/threat-management/201010/communicating-people-mental-illness-the-publics-guide

https://www.cdc-gov/mentalhealth

8. ***Learning to Calm the Storm:*** This is a two hour class on the basics of de-escalation techniques along with practical exercises to reinforce the needed skills. This course is important for all staff members and it provides CRITICAL instruction for how to deal with people who are "escalating." Remember, 60% of all of the attacks on churches since 1999 have been when there is no service going on.

9. ***Indicators of Violence:*** This is one hour class designed to provide practical instruction for teams to understand and identify indicators of violence in people. Developed by the FBI's Behavior Analysis Unit (BAU) and provides practical guidance for what to look for in potentially violent people.

10. ***The Ministry of Security:*** This is a one-hour class designed to provide practical ministry training for how Safety and Security team members can access and minister to hurting people. Of course, prayer must be your operating principal; before, during and after each service, prayer must be employed. We are the tip of the spear. We are targets of the enemy because we have committed to stand in the gap, to man the wall, to protect the flock. This course provides important instruction for how to listen, help and pray for those in need.

Check with your state to see what training is available to you. In SC, (our State) the State Law Enforcement Division (SLED) has established a training and certification program to standardize how private security groups, both paid and volunteer, function.

This Proprietary Security training, in South Carolina, authorizes each Certified "officer" with the same authority as a Deputy Sheriff on our church property. The training, divided into three parts, *"Basic"*, *"Plus"* and *"Firearms"* can be tailored to each volunteer according to the need and the assignment. This training lowers your liability and raises the "bar" for church security.

Establishing "Post Orders" will establish the what-to-do and what-not-to-do and give your Members guidelines for action and your Team Leaders will have a measuring tool to make certain that the Members are doing what they should be doing. Our Post Orders are based on the SCSLED curriculum that we use and are offered here as a guideline for your Team. Stay within the guidelines and stay out of trouble. Post orders establish the parameters of operation for your Team. Feel free to modify them to fit your mission.

"Post Orders"

These Post Orders are based on the (South Carolina Code of Laws, Title 40, Chapter 18), and shall be the guiding principal of the *(Insert your group name here)* Emergency Response (or, Security, or Safety) Team. *(In SC you can only use the word "security" if you have the state certification)*

Failure to act as required by these Post Orders is cause for disciplinary

action against you. *(This is your hammer for discipline.)*

Mission statement: The Mission of the Emergency Response Team (ERT) is to assist the contracted Police Officers (if you do this) assure a safe and peaceful place for the attendees of our Church to meet and to worship.

"We prayed to our God, and posted a Guard." Nehemiah 4:9

As a registered Private Security Officer you are under a duty to protect life and the property and the assets of our Church.

Your service and expertise are greatly valued. These Post Orders are to act as parameters for your activity as a Security Officer and a member of the Emergency Response Team Ministry.

1. Registration: All members, are to be trained to our church specifications to perform the specific activities detailed by the written emergency response policies. Annual re-certification is required.

2. Communication: When reporting for duty, members are to meet in the ERT Office (we call it the Kennel, where we raise champion Sheepdogs), report to the Team Leader for that service or event, sign in on the log sheet, and draw a radio, if available, that corresponds with the sign-in line on the radio/attendance log.

The **Red Lanyard** identifies you as a member of the ERT and is to be worn outside of the clothing unless otherwise directed by the Team Leader.

3. SLED training (or whatever you direct as minimum training) is to be completed at the earliest opportunity. The proof of training is to be carried on your person at all times when working at our church. Failure to do so will cause termination.

4. Ethics: All members of the ERT are to demonstrate good character and integrity commensurate with being a committed follower of Jesus Christ.

5. Professionalism: All ERT members will present themselves in a professional manner at all times in dress and deportment. (Appropriate dress and no flip-flops. (You can't run and you can't fight in them.)

6. Situational Awareness: While on duty each member will be aware of their surroundings, front, back, up, down, left and right. Anything that does not look right, given the surroundings of the church, is to be reported immediately to the duty Team Leader who will determine the need to follow up. When on duty, **do not** use your cell phone for anything but communication. (iPhone + iPad = iDistracted)

7. Observation: If a situation requires additional or concentrated observation, the Team Leader shall determine the degree and the number of personnel necessary to accomplish the observation. If required for an inconspicuous presentation, the Red Lanyard should be removed or hidden. Note the nearest camera position and report it to the Team Leader.

8. Law Enforcement Relations: The Law Enforcement Officers (LEO) are the primary responders to legal issues (trespass notices) and/or violent behavior. Good relationships with the LEO's assigned are vital to the conduct of our Mission.

The ERT shall act as force multipliers for the officers assigned to the church if needed and the LEO shall be included in any activity where suspicion of wrong-doing is observed or suspected.

9. Note Taking: All members shall carry a notebook and pen on their person when on duty and take copious notes of any incident. Who, What, Where, When and Date and Time are to be recorded. Complete, Clear, Concise, Correct, Contemporaneous.

10. Discovered Criminal Activity: Immediately secure the scene. The suspected activity shall be reported to the Team Leader and the LEO on duty immediately. The ERT member shall be able to articulate what he/she witnessed and have notes sufficient to complete a witnessed account of what was seen/heard. You have NO investigative authority. (Leave investigations to the police. They have to build the case justifying the arrest, not you.)

11. Crime Scene Preservation: In the case of a crime being perpetrated on Seacoast property, the member must be diligent in protecting the scene from any tampering or compromise until relieved by a Team Leader or LEO.

12. Workplace Violence: Any workplace violence is to be reported to the Team Leader and LEO immediately whether witnessed or reported. If witnessed a full report containing who, what, where, when and the time of occurrence is to be annotated in the duty log, an incident report completed, and LEO notified.

(In the case of crimes against children, a complete incident report must be completed and LEO notified immediately by law.).

13. Emergency Response: In case of an emergency requiring assistance, the Team Leader will dispatch the members necessary to handle the emergency. If you are not dispatched, <u>you are to remain at your assigned post.</u> Any and all emergency responses are to be logged into the duty log and annotated on an incident report.

If an ambulance or additional first response is required, the LEO on duty should make the request and any medical team members on duty should be notified. If they are not available, call 911 immediately.

14. Violent Threats: Any and all violent threats are to be reported to LEO, Team Leader, and logged. The report must include who the threat was directed to, what was said and where the incident occurred. Bomb Threats shall follow the DHS Guidelines, posted in the Kennel.

15. Training Documentation: SLED is adamant that all training records be up to date and accurate. It is the members responsibility to make certain that any and all training records and certificates be in their file and that the SLED ID card be carried on their person whenever they are working at Church. SLED will fine you for failing to do this. (It makes sense that you maintain a file on each member with any and all training documentation. If anything happens, the investigation authority will want to see all of it.)

16. Patrol Procedures: When reporting for duty the Team Leader will assign the member to a post, either fixed or flexible. These posts will vary depending on what is taking place during the duty period.

If the post is inside of the worship center during a service, the member will remain on that post for the duration of the service.

If the post is a "roaming" assignment, the member will check each door, classroom, and hallway, closet and storage room. They should make eye contact with each teacher and/or staff member/volunteer so that they know that the ERT is there if needed. It is vital that a friendly, open appearance be presented by all members while on duty. "Wary as snakes, harmless as doves," should guide our activities when on duty. We are not there to intimidate, but to serve.

17. Vehicle Operations: If the vehicle used by Facilities is used as a patrol vehicle, the "Security" signage, stored in the vehicle, MUST be displayed or we are in violation of the law. Before operating this vehicle you must be qualified by Facilities for safe and effective operation.

18. Reasonable Suspicion: If a crime is suspected, reasonable suspicion is required before any action is taken. Notify the Team Leader and LEO before taking any action.

19. Probable Cause: The **Fourth Amendment** of the U.S. Constitution provides, "That the right of the people to be secure in their persons, houses, papers and effect against unreasonable search and seizure shall not be violated but upon probable cause, supported by oath or affirmation, and particularly describing the place and persons to be seized." (So be careful when you check a backpack or a parcel.)

20. Arrest: Although (SLED Proprietary Security Certification) grants the authority to place a person under arrest, the Security team **WILL NOT** exercise this authority, but will notify the nearest LEO for that action and assist in any way that is deemed necessary.

21. Transportation of Prisoners: Any and all transportation of prisoners will be the sole responsibility of Law Enforcement.

22. Terry Stop: In Terry v. Ohio, the Supreme Court allowed that a suspicious person could be stopped, handcuffed for officer safety, and frisked without placing the person under arrest. Security will notify LEO for this action.

23. Use of Force: The Use of Force Continuum is clear in what is necessary when force is employed. Familiarize yourself with the "Use of Force" continuum posted on the Kennel wall. In any and all cases, the Team Leader and LEO must be alerted.

24. Testimony: You must be able to articulate the Who, What, Where, When and How in any case or situation which requires your assistance and indicates the need for an incident report.

25. Handling Difficult People: Prayer is the key to our success in our mission. When possible, a Pastor or Prayer Team member should be employed. If you sense violence could erupt, contact the Team Leader and a LEO immediately. Call 911 if necessary.

26. Handcuffs, Baton, Capstun: Equipment or devices for which you have not successfully completed training adequate to insure the safe, proper and accurate use of such equipment shall not be used. Documentation of appropriate training must be in the members file.

27. Firearms: State certification must be completed as the base line. Additional certification by the Firearms Instructor Team is required to be armed on church property. Each certified member must also carry liability insurance provided by membership in the USCCA (www.USCCA.com). A copy of the membership card is to be placed in the members file.

Each qualified member must practice monthly and note the date of the practice in the Range Book in the Kennel in order to continue to carry.

Active Shooter: Each Member must complete the on-line training in Active Shooter response by ALICE as soon as it is sent via email. The link will be sent and any IT issues can be resolved by contacting http://www.ALICEtraining.com. The certificate of completion is to be placed in the members file. (The cost of this program is about $10.00 per person. If you want to be an instructor, ALICE offers programs frequently.)

28. Qualifications: Additional qualifications in martial arts, firearms, etc., are to be noted in the members file along with any appropriate certificates.

29. Service: Each Member is expected to attend Worship Services on a regular basis as Members of Seacoast Church and to serve the ERT at a minimum of two weekend services (Saturday or Sunday) per month.

30. Termination: Violation of any of the above is reason for termination from the ERT.

31. Any issues not expressly covered above should be directed by common sense. When in doubt, contact the Team Leader on duty or the nearest LEO.

(I encourage you to have each Member sign and date. Do this every year so that there are no questions about what is expected. It will keep you out of trouble should trouble develop.)

I have read and fully understand the above Post Orders and agree to follow them without deviation.

Date:_____

_____   _____
Print Your Name

Rings of Security

Look at establishing rings of security. History shows that <u>75% of the attacks on churches begin on the parking lot</u> we incorporate our Parking Team into our training as the first ring. Greeters and Ushers are also welcome into our training as ring two and the ERT acts as ring three. Eyes and Ears are our most important tool, employ all of them.

Reports: For insurance and legal purposes, document <u>everything</u> that you do. Sheepdog Church Security has developed several report forms. They are included here for your review. You can download them at the <u>sheepdogchurchsecurity.com</u> website.

I do pray that this booklet helps you to initiate or refine your church security program. It does not cover every situation, but may provide a basis for what you need to know going forward. Please let me know if this helps or how I can assist you further.

I encourage you to join the Faith Based Security Network (FBSN) to stay current with what is happening in our (your) ministry. Go to <u>carl@fbsnamerica.com</u> for info.

A list of reading material would include:

<u>Left of Bang</u>, by Van Horn and Riley
<u>The Gift of Fear</u>, by Gavin DeBecker
<u>Evil Invades the Sanctuary</u>, by Carl Chinn
<u>On Killing</u>, by LTC David Grossman, USA, (Ret)
<u>Two Seconds</u>, by Gavin DeBecker
<u>Defending the Flock</u>, by Kris Moloney
<u>The Ideal Team Player</u> by Patrick Lencioni
<u>Mental Health First Aid,</u> www.MentalHealthFirst**aid.org**

I am available to assist you in any way. My contact information is:

Bill Gadol
Director, Seacoast Security
Seacoast Church, Mt. Pleasant (SC) campus
billgadol@seacoast.org
wgadol@gmail.com

About the Author:

Bill Gadol has served as a U.S. Army Military Police Supervisor, a Firefighter/Paramedic and a corporate emergency medical systems consultant to the FBI, U.S. Secret Service, National Football league, and Special Operations commands for all of the U.S. Armed Forces. He is a former Senior Instructor for EMT's, an Instructor Trainer for CPR for the American Heart Association, an Instructor Trainer for Basic and Advanced First Aid for the American Red Cross, and a Reserve Deputy Sheriff assigned to the Federal Anti-Terrorism Task Force. He is currently a Life Member of the Special Operations Medical Association, an Instructor for ALICE (Active Shooter Program), the South Carolina State Law Enforcement Division (SCSLED) for the Proprietary Security program, SCSLED Firearms Instructor, CWP Instructor and a member of Infragard.. He serves as an Elder and as the Director of Security for Seacoast Church, Mt. Pleasant, SC.

He can be reached via email at wgadol@gmail.com or at P.O. Box 51648, Summerville, SC 29485.

Made in the USA
Monee, IL
26 October 2021